RESET

Learn How to Grow Money and Build a Legacy

Erica Hill

Published by:

Create Your Fab, LLC
1455 Lincoln Parkway E
Dunwoody, GA 30346

For general information or other products or services, contact
Erica Hill at hello@createyourfab.com or www.createyourfab.com

Dedication

Imagine being the first person in your family to leave generational wealth. Imagine leaving a legacy. Imagine leaving a family playbook where the next three generations will be taken care of financially because you paved the way. How could this change your family's last name?

Wealth, as we have discovered, results from the financial strategies and habits we live by every day. The wealthy operate by a different playbook. They use a two-hundred-year-old strategy to eliminate debt, grow their wealth, minimize taxation, and leave a legacy to their heirs.

This book was written to inspire and educate families on the secrets that the wealthy have been using for centuries to grow their money and leave generational wealth.

Let's go . . .
Xoxo, Erica

Disclaimer

This book has been written solely for informational and educational purposes. No content constitutes professional or individual-specific financial advice. While best efforts were employed when writing this book to include accurate, verifiable content, the author or anyone else who may have been involved in any way in the preparation of this book makes no representations or warranties of any kind. It assumes no liabilities as related to the accuracy or completeness of the information presented.

The author and all parties involved in the preparation of this book shall not be held liable for any loss or damages caused or alleged to have been caused, directly or indirectly, by the information presented herein.

Every individual's financial situation is unique, and the information and strategies in this book speak to the book's audience in general and may not apply to your specific situation.

Table of Contents

Introduction

"**F**ormal education will make you a living; self-education will make you a fortune"- Jim Rohn.

Oh, how true this is. For me, I had to learn a hard lesson about money. The schools that I attended did not teach me about money, so I had to learn by watching the adults around me (and they weren't good with money), so guess what?

I wasn't good with money.

I grew up in a low- to middle-class family. My parents divorced when I was ten, and I went to live with my grandmother, but my parents remained a part of my life. I would see my father in the summers because he lived in a different state, and I would see my mom regularly because we lived in the same city.

My mom had four children, and when my parents divorced, my grandmother decided to help raise the oldest two (my sister and me). If you were on the outside looking in, you would think that my sister and I had the best of everything because, while my grandmother made sure that we were well dressed, well fed, and well educated, we lacked something important—an education regarding handling finances.

Yes, we were educated according to the school system. We graduated from high school, and I went on to get a college degree from Clark Atlanta University, but we lacked education about being good stewards of our money.

For some reason, everyone forgot this part. No one sat down and taught me about money. My grandmother didn't teach me; my parents didn't teach me; the schools didn't teach me; the university that I graduated from didn't teach me. If someone had taught me at an early age the *secrets* that I will share in this book, I guarantee you that I would be a billionaire. Instead, I was taught to go to college, get a degree and you will make more money. The funny part was this: no one taught me what to do with the money once I made it. So, I listened. I was very obedient.

I graduated with a degree in Business Finance, but as I walked across the stage to get my degree, bad credit walked with me. In my sophomore year in college, students were offered credit cards.

When I got approved for my card, I went shopping at the mall. I maxed that card out. Did I forget to mention that I didn't have a job? So, guess what happened . . .

By the age of twenty, I ended up with bad credit.

In the financial industry the first thing prospective employers do is check your credit.

It took four years to get a college degree and seven years to clean up my credit.

I found a job working at a finance company, but I still had not learned how to be a good steward of my money, and this was my first real job. When I got paid, I would go shopping. I didn't cook, so I ate out a lot. I loved to be entertained, so I was forever going to various social events. I could genuinely say that I would go out of control until it was time to pay my bills, and then I didn't have enough money. The fun feelings quickly turned into panic, fear, anxiety, stress, depression (to name a few). I started to feel like a failure. When I looked at my bank account and saw insufficient funds, I felt worse. I would pay some bills now; then I had to wait until the next paycheck to pay other bills. I always ended up in the *red*. This continued for at least three years. For some reason, I could not figure out how to get off this financial rollercoaster. I saw my friends with designer handbags and clothes, so I wanted them.

I didn't want to feel *less than* by not having the things that they had. Let's face it. We all had degrees. When they went on vacation, I wanted to go too.

I found myself always wanting to be a part of the in *crowd*. It seemed that material things brought my friends happiness, and I wanted to be happy too. They could go to a club, spend lots of money and have fun so I wanted to do the same things. My identity became wrapped around material things and less around things of substance.

To make matters worse, my boyfriend came from a privileged upbringing, so he also bought expensive things. He was forever showering me with gifts, and I wanted to do the same thing for him. He wouldn't accept inexpensive items.

If it didn't cost a certain amount, he didn't want it. So, hey. I had a facade to keep up. I started noticing, though, that the things that I thought were supposed to bring me happiness started to do anything but that. I was always depressed, stressed, worried, and fearful. I got to the point where the only things that I wanted to do was eat and sleep.

I started to put on weight, and then I started to with-draw from people. The fun times became far and few between. The feelings grew worse when I looked at my bank account and had no money saved. I started to feel like a loser. I would go to work, and my co-workers would be talking about the things that they did over the weekend, and my story would be like, "Yeah, I didn't do anything. I just slept." Then, one day it hit me . . . I had fallen into a deep depression, and it all stemmed from my financial situation, or so I thought. Somewhere and somehow, *I had lost me.* I no longer was this fun-go-lucky person. I could not allow this to con-tinue, so I started to seek counsel through prayer. I was taught that when everything else fails, take it to God, and this is what I did. I went to church more, and I con-nected to the Word (my Bible). As my faith grew stron-ger, I noticed that my situation started to change, and my outlook on life also started to shift. I no longer saw myself as the victim but as the conqueror. I also started to change my circle of friends, including the guy that I was dating. I started to want more for myself. I quit my job and found a better one in the mortgage indus-try. I saw people my age buying houses. Never before was home ownership something that I thought about, but when I was put into an environment where this was common, it became important to me as well. I felt like: If Sallie can buy a home, so can I. I started doing everything that I needed to do to purchase a home. The first thing was to work on my mindset. I put systems in place that would allow me to become a homeowner and this included improving my credit and saving for a down payment. I created a budget, and I would not go outside of it no matter what. The old habits of going out of control no longer existed, but I would treat myself to something nice at least once a month. I didn't want to feel like I was depriving myself; however, I did not accumulate more debt. I knew that my debt-to-income ratio had to stay within reason to get approved for my house. The days of living paycheck to paycheck had ended.

I always felt I would not be so stressed if I made more money, but the issue was not the amount of money that I was *making*. The issue was the amount of money that I was *spending*. I would see people who made less money buying a house. It was because they were good stewards of their money. They were not carrying the debt that I was carrying.

It also became apparent that my self-worth was not based on material things. Looking at my material things that I considered important—none of them would help me to purchase a home. I mean, these were not appreciating assets. They were not assets at all. They were liabilities. I also began to study the patterns of wealthy people. People like Warren Buffet, Bill

Gates, Michael Bloomberg, Oprah Winfrey, Bob Johnson, and Sheila Johnson (just to name a few). I started to understand that the real secret to wealth is having multiple streams of income and saving and investing your money. I started to change my circle of friends. I no longer surrounded myself with people who talked about how much money they were going to spend but with people who talked about how much money they were going to invest.

Chapter One

Money Road Blocks

I realized that as a child; I heard a lot of negative things about money. Things like, "Money doesn't grow on trees, and we can't afford this, or we can't afford that, or you have to work hard to make money." All of the conversations about money were negative, and I developed a lack and scarcity mindset. Everything that I did, from spending more than I earned, not keeping an eye on my money, living paycheck to paycheck, and so on, were acts of someone with a poverty mindset. No one in my immediate family was extremely wealthy, so I didn't think being wealthy was possible. *But once I became aware* of my poverty mindset and changed it to an abundant mindset, I started to build generational wealth. I purchased my first home at the age of 27.

I became a real estate investor at the age of 32 and purchased two more properties. I opened a mortgage company at the age of 37. I realized that you could change any gloomy situation. All it takes is the right mindset, a plan, and action. So here we go!

How to Develop a Mindset of Wealth

If you are a part of the 99%, you probably have not developed a mindset of wealth; the reason is that most people believe you must have a job. Every wealthy person knows that you will never become wealthy from working a j.o.b. (just over broke). Almost every wealthy person is an entrepreneur and has a product or service that people want. And/or he or she has created multiple income streams.

Wealth is power! If you are like most people, you don't believe that you have power. You believe that the powers that be are in control, and the rest of us are victims of the system.

This is a poverty mindset, and it is often entrained and passed from one generation to the next.

Keep in mind that money does not equal wealth. Many people have plenty of money, but still carry around the poverty mentality of "not enough." They may hold onto their money, but they are afraid to spend, so they hoard money. Then, some spend it so irresponsibly that they lose it and find themselves at square one again.

Human beings follow through on who they believe they are. If you believe that you are unworthy of wealth, and you win the lottery for 100 million dollars; you will find a way to lose it either by unconsciously creating situations of hardship, emergency, or disaster, or you will frivolously waste it and watch it slip through your fingers like water.

We hear stories about poor people who win the lottery, and in two years, they are back where they started.

If we understand that money is nothing more than energy, we will know that we attract or repel money. Some people are good at attracting money, and some are good at repelling it.

Ways to Improve Your Relationship with Money

1. Understand that we live in an abundant universe and our natural state of being is abundance.

Abundance in health, happiness, and wealth. The Universe lacks nothing, and there is only one stream. There isn't a stream of abundance and a stream of lack. We are either going with the stream or against it, and when we go against it; we feel lack. When we move in congruency with the stream, we feel abundance. You've heard the term "go with the flow"? Wealthy people have mastered this. When they get an idea or hunch, they go with it, and it always leads to an abundant outcome.

2. Understand that energy moves by nature, and if money is energy, it must move in and out.

Trying to hold onto money with the belief that it's not enough or hard to come by only keeps it from flowing to you. Therefore, you can start by being joyful when you pay your bills or pay for a service. Don't begrudge when paying for things, because you are signaling the Universe that you don't believe more is coming. Wealthy people never wonder if they will get more money because they understand that they can attract more, and they do so.

3. Visualize money coming into your experience from multiple sources.

See money flowing to you like water flowing downhill, and experience what it feels like to have an endless supply of money and resources in your possession. Wealthy people see the unseen before it shows up. People with money look into the future and experience the feeling of having the lifestyle they desire, and they manifest it. A lot of people dismiss this intangible process because they don't believe it works, just as they don't believe they can be wealthy; their beliefs prove them right.

Chapter Two

How Money Works

Everything we want to create in our business and personal lives begins with money. Renowned American businessman and author Zig Ziglar put it best when he said, "Money isn't everything, but it's reasonably close to oxygen on the 'got to have it' scale."

The world is full of plans, gurus, and clutter that keep us in the dark about our money. It doesn't help that we have been unintentionally misled to think that money is wrong or that we're too dumb to understand how to make, save, and grow it (i.e., that we need to pay and trust someone else to do that for us). The whole conversation in this book is about money--how money flows, what money does, and what you do with money--because what you don't know is hurting you. Global financial Educator Robert Kiyosaki says, "The big shift must come in education, not only in what we teach but how we teach." Let's talk about what money is and how it works. Simply put, money is a means of exchange for goods and services. We exchange money for food, food for money, money for cars, cars for money, money for houses, houses for money, money for vacations, and vacations for money.

Tony Robbins says, "At its core, money is about power. We've all seen how money can have the power to create or the power to destroy." He says, "One thing is for sure: you either use it or it will use you."

In his book, *Second Chance: for Your Money, Your Life, and Our World*, Robert Kiyosaki says that measuring wealth in money will cause "the rich to become the new poor." He points out several reasons:

1. "money is no longer money."

2. "knowledge is the new money."

3. the low and middle class of today have the opportunity to "become the new rich of tomorrow."

Kiyosaki makes the bold statement that "our wealth is stolen via our money."

He points out three areas where our money is disappearing:

1. **Taxes** – The value of our labor is stolen through taxes.

2. **Inflation** – Prices increase when the government prints money.

3. **Savings** – As Kiyosaki says, "Savers are losers" because banks steal savers' wealth via the "fractional reserve system" banking process (a form of printing money). Suppose knowledge is the new money, and execution is really power. In that case, this book is going to give you the power to reclaim control of your money—your income-producing and wealth-building power—so that you can live the lifestyle you want, have the retirement you want, and leave the legacy you want.

Illusions of Retirement Freedom

Thirty-four million baby boomers are currently in retirement. The remaining seventy million baby boomers are getting ready to retire, and almost half of Americans approaching retirement have little to nothing saved. When we have something saved, and we put our money into retirement accounts, we give away our money (and our power) to those who are willing to handle these accounts for us. The trouble is that we don't know if they've done an excellent job until it may be too late.

What do we know about our retirement accounts? You likely know whether the money goes up or down, based on your quarterly statements. You also may know whether your money is invested in a low-, moderate-, or high-risk category. Other than that, most people don't know anything about what their money is doing. In his book, MONEY *Master the Game*, Tony Robbins states that "Polls show that fewer than one in four trusts the financial system—with good reason!"

Robert Kiyosaki says, "Today, millions of Americans, through their 401(k)s and IRAs, blindly turn their money over to people they do not know or trust. They follow the instructions of parrots, repeating what they have been told to say. That's a risky proposition. When you put your money into these government-sponsored accounts; you put your trust and your money into someone else's hands without a guarantee of what will happen to your funds within the accounts. There is no protection of your funds. If Wall Street sinks into the New York Harbor what will happen to your money?

Most people don't even know that their 401k is a

government-sponsored plan. The most dangerous thing you can do with money is put it into a government-sponsored plan.

The reason is that when you put your money into 401(k)s and IRAs, you will get your money later—years down the road. You have to lock your money away for years before you can use it.

You cannot get to your money without paying penalties and taxes until you turn 59½. The reality is that if you are contributing to a 401(k), an IRA, or another qualified plan, you might as well forget about your money since you can't touch it today or tomorrow. The saying, "Out of sight, out of mind" is accurate. You also, give up the opportunity to use your money today, while the value of the dollar is still substantial. This means you lose the opportunity of putting the money toward your house, your car, your business, or your lifestyle. You are also forced to pay taxes on that money. Let's say that you have $100,000 in a 401k. When you withdraw those funds (depending on your age) you will pay between 20-30% taxes. So, you will end up with $70,000 or $80,000 instead of $100,000.

Here's a critical question: Is a dollar worth more today or in the future? The answer is *Today*. You could buy more candy bars twenty years ago for $1 than you can today.

If you go to the grocery store today and buy milk, a steak, and a loaf of bread, would you wait twenty years to drink that milk and eat that steak and bread? Of course not. This is the source of our pain and struggle around money and what we've been taught to believe. When you put money in a government- or employer-sponsored retirement plan--a 401(k), an IRA, or another qualified plan--you're buying a loaf of bread and putting it in the freezer. In, say, twenty years, you open the freezer and see two loaves of bread (representing your money). Is that second loaf of bread any good? No, it's freezer burned! Tomorrow's dollars will never be worth what they are today.

Robert Kiyosaki explains this by saying, "The opposite of saving is known as the 'velocity of money.' Most people 'park' their money where they save or invest for retirement. Smart people keep their money moving. When you park your money, your money loses value. When you keep your money moving, your money increases in value."

The second critical question is this: Are taxes going to go up or down? Like most everything else, taxes go up, and even if they don't go up, you will be taxed on more goods (of more significant cost) than you were in the past. Robert Kiyosaki says, "Inflation is good for debtors and bad for savers, which is why savers are losers."

The third critical question is as follows: Would you rather pay taxes on the seed or the harvest? In other words, do you want to pay tax on the money you invest (the small amount) or the money you make (the massive amount)?

The small amount, right? When you invest in retirement plans; you violate your desires because you are being taxed on your harvest (the large future amount). When you take the money out, that money will be taxed. The only thing you're avoiding by taking your money out at the proper age is the penalty.

We've been taught to give away our good dollars today and get paid back with weaker dollars in the future.

By being your own banking system, versus relying on traditional investment methods, you no longer have to lock up your cash; you no longer have to turn over control to someone else; you can continue to spend on your lifestyle and business, and you can realize growth is guaranteed from day one. R. Nelson Nash says, "There are only two income sources — people at work and money at work." You can either continue to work hard and turn your hard-earned dollars over to someone else to control, or you can choose to think differently, become your bank, and make your money work for you. It's time to choose to control your money from the beginning and every day after that. Becoming Your

Bank, also known as the Infinite Banking Concept, is built upon three foundational principles for your life and your money.

Three Banking Concepts

1. **Pay Yourself First**. We think we know it, but it can be hard to do. It's easy to give our money to the car people, the house people, the TV people, the electricity people, the grocery people, the school people, the investment guy. It's time to keep your money rather than giving it away.

2. **Pay Yourself with Interest**. Millionaires understand that using their money involves a premium and privilege. When you become your bank, you're going to learn to treat your money like the bank's money. When you borrow money, you pay it back with interest. If money flows out of your banking system, money should be put back to replace it.

3. **Recapture What You Spend**. Recapturing and recycling the money you spend is one of the most powerful processes you'll learn. You can get back the money you spend on cars, your home, and even your charitable giving and taxes while building your wealth and legacy. That's what Becoming Your Own Bank is about!

To become your bank, recycle and recapture the interest you're paying everyone else, and regain full control of your finances; we need to investigate the system itself—how banks work and what we can learn from them.

Chapter Three

How Banks Work

Say you have $100,000. What do you do with it? You deposit it in the bank. For example, say that you've found a suitable bank account that pays 4% interest. When you put money into the bank, that money becomes a liability to the bank, because they owe you interest. Remember that anything that depletes cash flow is a liability. The bank then takes your money and turns it into an asset by loaning it to others. Loans are assets to banks because loans make money for banks; they create cash flow.

Banks are in the money business—the lending business. The money you put into your bank account gets loaned back to you or to someone else to buy a house, a car, etc. The banks bring money in and move it out continuously — keeping the money in motion, and they do so in a way that is favorable to them from a cash-flow perspective. If you are earning that 4% mentioned above on the money in your account and your bank is loaning that money to you or (someone else) at an interest rate of 7%, (you or that someone else) is expected to pay the bank back the full amount of the loan, plus the 7% interest. The bank is in full control of the transaction and benefits by creating the loan — the asset.

Regardless of what you want to borrow money for — a car, house remodeling, a new deck, a swimming pool, a boat — you are expected to pay back the loan plus interest.

Therefore, if you take an 8% loan to buy a car, you have to pay back the loan's full amount, plus the 8% interest. If you want to get a home equity line, borrowing money from the bank at say 9%, you pay back the amount of your loan, plus the 9% interest. If you take out a debt consolidation loan at, say, 12%, and use it to pay off your credit cards, you pay off all your credit cards, and then the loan has to be paid back to the bank plus the 12% interest.

Money is always going back into the banking system, and the bank is in control, as they are continuously moving money in and out. What if I told you that the bank made 500% more than you did with the 4% interest you earned on the money you placed in the bank account through this process? Let's look at the math:

- If you are earning 4% and the bank is lending it to you or someone else as a homebuyer at 7%, the bank makes 3% more.

- If you are earning 4% and the bank is lending it to you or someone else to buy a car at 8%, the bank is making 4% more.

- If you are earning 4% and the bank is lending it to you or someone else to do a home remodel at 9%, the bank makes 5% more.

- If you are earning 4% and the bank is lending it to you or someone else to consolidate debt at 12%, the bank makes 8% more.

- 3% + 4% + 5% + 8% = 20% . . . that's 20% more than you make, but there's more to this equation. If you make $4 on every $100 and the bank makes $20, they make five times, or 500%, more than you make!

Look at how many banks there are. Their buildings are typically the loveliest in town. By putting money into bank accounts and taking out bank loans, you pay for those buildings. The bank is in control of your money, and they are taking a minimal risk and using your money to loan to others. To further protect themselves, the higher risk you are, the higher the interest rate you will have to pay, and if you are too high a risk, the banks won't lend to you.

Banks make between 400% and 1,300% on the money you put in and leave there every year. The bank's annual report will show you how much they are making on the money you have there. Rarely, if ever, has this number been below 400%.20

The Power of Compound Interest

Compound interest is the interest on a loan or deposit calculated based on both the initial principal and the accumulated interest. When you deposit money in a savings account or a similar account, you'll usually receive interest based on the amount that you deposited.

So, let's go over a quick rule called "the rule of 72." The rule of 72 is the interest rate divided by 72 and it tells you how long it takes to double your money. For example, if you were 29 and you had $10K in a savings account that was paying 1% interest, you would divide 72/1. It would take 72 years for your money to double. You would be 101 years old before you doubled your money to $20K.

This is the phase where you can be making money in your sleep, but the best way to do this is to have multiple investment vehicles that utilize compound interest.

Do you believe in compound interest? The only way compound interest works is if your money is sitting still — remaining in the same place. If you remove your money from the bank, it no longer earns compound interest.

Motion is a natural law of the universe. You wouldn't want to eat a fish you caught from a stagnant pond, would you? When we think of one business that uses compound interest, the most common answer is a bank.

In all actuality, banks do not use compound interest themselves. They pay you compound interest and charge you compound interest, though they do not use it themselves.

Say you make a broad mark with a yellow highlighter on a $20 bill, initial it, and take it to the bank. If you return to the bank in a month to retrieve that same $20 bill, you will not get it back. The bank has not kept your money in a particular little black box for you. You will not ever retrieve that particular $20 bill — not in a day, not in a week, not in a month. Why? Because as we mentioned earlier, banks are in the business of lending money, and because of this, they keep their money in motion.

No real businesses have money sitting still to build compound interest. If a car dealer doesn't move cars, they don't make money. If a grocery store doesn't move the products off their shelves, they don't make money. All the institutions that promote compound interest—banks, Wall Street, mutual funds, and insurance companies--tell us to park our money with them, but they don't park the money!

Institutions keep money in motion, using it to earn interest (cashflow) for themselves. In the financial world, we continually hear about how good compound interest is. If this is the case, why aren't these larger institutions using it? It all comes down to how we use uninterrupted compound interest to create our wealth. In his book, *MONEY Master the Game,* Tony Robbins speaks of his interview with Burton Malkiel, the man behind index funds. An index fund is a mutual fund or exchange-traded fund designed to follow certain preset rules so that the fund can track a specified basket of underlying investments. Robbins asked Malkiel, "What's the biggest misstep most of us make right from the start?"

Malkiel said, "The majority of investors fail to take full advantage of the incredible power of compounding— the multiplying power of growth times growth." The money you put into a permanent life insurance policy is put to work by the insurance company, so they are ensuring the compounding benefits of your policy value's growth. At the same time, you get to act like the banks and keep your money in motion by taking out loans from the insurance company's general fund. More about this in the next chapter.

Become Your Own Bank

All of us have the power to change our financial trajectory by stepping outside of the norm and adding a straightforward step to our financial life: becoming our bank. Founder of the Infinite Banking Concept™ R. Nelson Nash says, "When you own the capital, you have the control." He also says, "There has got to be some honest introspection at this point, and a commitment to 'get out of financial prison' must be a burning passion. This is going to require a change in priorities in life, and recognizing that controlling the banking function personally is the essential thing that can be done in your financial world."

Those who have realized the most significant financial success know that our wealth results from the financial habits and strategies we live by. Wealthy people use a two-hundred-year-old strategy to eliminate debt; they grow their wealth, minimize taxation, and leave a legacy to their heirs. What the wealthy know and do centers around the banking function—controlling their environment. Robert Kiyosaki, Tony Robbins, and R. Nelson Nash talk about this secret. Walt Disney used it to build Disney World. Ray Kroc used it to build the McDonald's franchise. Sears and J. C. Penney have similar founding stories. The Infinite Banking Concept is founded upon this little-known but long-standing and exponentially powerful strategy which is used by the top 5%.

R. Nelson Nash says, "Everyone should be in two businesses—the one in which you make your living, and the other should be the banking business that finances whatever you do for a living. Of the two businesses, banking is the most important." He defines the Infinite Banking Concept™, which he founded in the 1980s, as "an exercise in imagination, reason, logic, and prophecy. . . It is about recovering the interest that one normally pays to some banking institution and then lending it to others so that the policy owner makes what a banking institution does. It is like building an environment in the airplane world where you have a perpetual 'tailwind' instead of a perpetual 'headwind.'"

Before reading this book, you may have thought that it was impossible to control the environment in which your investments sit . . . With the Infinite Banking Concept--the modern-day, elaborate process of creating your banking system--you become the owner and the banker, and you have full control over how your money is used.

This is about taking responsibility for your wealth and your legacy, and not leaving it in the hands of the banks, investment companies, and the government. Inside this book is the education, understanding, and process you need to change your financial trajectory and reclaim control of your financial future. You must become your banker so that you can truly build wealth and legacy. This strategy will change your financial destiny and outline the marathon thinking and requirements to help you become wealthy. Once you free yourself from financial slavery and regain control of your finances, you can generate more money for the following:

- Retirement

- Lifestyle

- Family

- Business

- Legacy

You can have full control of your financial future and how your money is used today. It sounds too good to be true, only because most people don't understand how it works. We will help you fully understand how the Infinite Banking Concept works and show you that it is, in fact, not too good to be true. We'll give you the process to keep control and ownership of your capital because we believe that change, for the better, only happens when we are willing to speak up.

Financial educator and founder of Rich Global LLC and the Rich Dad Company, Robert Kiyosaki, also teaches the Infinite Banking Concept through his work. He believes in personal responsibility and "changing the things we can change and control." In *Second Chance: for Your Money, Your Life, and Our World* — he argues that "many people need a second chance to rethink what they work for." He says, "Each of us has the power to change ourselves. And the easiest — and often most powerful — a change we can make is through education."

Tony Robbins, the nation's top life and business strategist, says, "Contrary to popular wisdom, knowledge is not power — it's potential power. Knowledge is not mastery. Execution is mastery." When we think we know it all, we stop learning, and yet we do not know what we've never been taught. The most significant financial knowledge is not taught; it's sought out. You will step into your power and your wealth by seeking out, understanding, and executing the financial truths delivered in this book.

Conclusion

How to Build a Legacy

There is no magic for building a solid financial foundation as there is no magic to losing weight. You eat right and exercise more. That will triumph over any special diet or pill. Likewise, no financial professional can help a person who spends more than he or she earns.

The old way of thinking--getting a good job, working until 65, and retiring happily--is over. Nowadays, it is important to be more proactive in thinking about making money.

Whether you stay a few more hours overtime, get a second job, work part-time, freelance, or start a business, you can use your unique skills and know how to make money. Many successful stories in business came from things people started in their garage or from their favorite hobbies.

If you look for it, you'll find it. Make it a mission to change your family's future.

1. Increase your cash flow. Make more money when you can, while you can. Have multiple streams of income.

2. Spend less. Cut your expenses. It's not how much you earn that counts. It's what you keep. Save 5, 10, 15% of your income.

3. Reduce your debt and liabilities. Interest on the debt will interfere with your goal for long-term asset accumulation.

4. Understand how money works. I covered this briefly earlier in the book. It will help you. Learn how to make money work for you.

5. Have a financial goal. Set up a plan of action

   • Take care of your responsibilities. Have proper protection by making sure that you have life insurance for yourself and your family outside of having life insurance at your job.

- Build wealth. Start to save. It's not how much. It's how disciplined you are. Start with a small amount and increase it gradually.

6. Set up the proper estate plan. Most people think estate planning is for rich people. But in fact, everyone has an estate. Your estate is everything you own minus your debt, such as your house, car, money in the bank, family heirlooms, etc. A will or trust is a tool to organize how you want your estate distributed when you pass away.

7. Embrace change and expect to succeed.

   - Change your habits. Not only can you change the way you think, but you must change your habits. Two things that can make significant changes in your life are the books you read and the people you meet.

Don't spend time with the wrong crowd. If you want to be successful, move to a better environment. Associate with successful people.

A better environment will help provide better thinking and better solutions.

- Expect to succeed.

You don't win or lose overnight. You win or lose by degree. If you want to win, make your way back toward winning, step by step, and follow through to completion. Expect to succeed. You are special. You know that you are somebody. And you can do a lot of great things. You're the head of the family. You're the captain of your ship.

Set sail, feel the wind, enjoy the journey.

References

Resources

1. R. Nelson Nash, Becoming Your Own Banker: Unlock the Infinite Banking Concept, Infinite Banking Concepts, 2009.

2. R. Nelson Nash, Becoming Your Own Banker: Unlock the Infinite Banking Concept, Infinite Banking Concepts, 2009.

3. Robert Kiyosaki, Second Chance: For Your Money, Your Life, and Our World, Plata Publishing, 2015.

4. U.S. Government Accountability Office, "Understanding The Debt", https://www.gao.gov/americas_fiscal_future?t=feder al_debt

5. R. Nelson Nash, Becoming Your Own Banker: Unlock the Infinite Banking Concept, The Infinite Banking Concepts, 2009. 6 Trading Economics, "United States Personal Savings Rate"https://tradingeconomics.com/united-states/personal-savings.

6. Trading Economics, "United States Personal Savings Rate"https://tradingeconomics.com/unitedstates/personal-savings.

7. Tony Robbins, MONEY Master the Game: 7 Simple Steps to Financial Freedom, Simon & Schuster, 2014, page 3.

8. Tony Robbins, MONEY Master the Game: 7 Simple Steps to Financial Freedom, Simon & Schuster, 2014, page 4.

9. Robert Kiyosaki, Second Chance: For Your Money, Your Life, and Our World, Plata Publishing, 2015, page 8-9.

10. Bob Pisani, CNBC, "Baby boomers face retirement crisis — little savings, high health costs and unrealistic expectations," April 2019 https://www.cnbc.com/2019/04/09/baby-boomersface -retirement-crisis-little-savings-high-health-costsand-unrealistic-expectations.html.

11. Annie Nova, CNBC, "Baby boomers face more risks to their retirement than previous generations," November 7, 2018 https://www.cnbc.com/2018/11/07/one-third-of-

12. Ben Steverman, Bloomberg, "Half of Older Americans Have Nothing in Retirement Savings," March 26, 2019 https://www.bloomberg.com/news/articles/2019-03-26/almost-half-of-older-americans-have-zero-in-retirement-savings.

13. Tony Robbins, MONEY Master the Game: 7 Simple Steps to Financial Freedom, Simon & Schuster, 2014, page 6.

14. Robert Kiyosaki, Second Chance: For Your Money, Your Life, and Our World, Plata Publishing, 2015, page 317.

15. "A record 7 million Americans are 3 months behind on their car payments, a red flag for the economy," The Washington Post, February 12, 2019, https://www.washingtonpost.com/business/2019/0 2/12/record-million-americans-are-months-behindtheir-car-payments-red-flag-economy/.

16. R Nelson Nash, Becoming Your Own Banker: Unlock the Infinite Banking Concept, Infinite Banking Concepts, 2009, page 17. "This seems

to be the current situation that doesn't change all much."140 Endnotes 141

17. Tony Robbins, Money: Master the Game: 7 Simple Steps to Financial Freedom, Simon & Schuster, 2014, page 50.

18. R. Nelson Nash, Building Your Warehouse of Wealth, Infinite Banking Concept™, LLC, 2000 (2012).

19. Tony Robbins, MONEY Master the Game: 7 Simple Steps to Financial Freedom, Simon & Schuster, 2014, page 56

20. R. Nelson Nash, Becoming Your Own Banker: Unlock the Infinite Banking Concept, Infinite Banking Concepts, 2009.

21. Federal Reserve Bank of New York, "Household Debt and Creditor Report," https://www. newyorkfed.org/microeconomics/hhdc. html.

22. Tony Robbins, MONEY Master the Game: 7 Simple Steps to Financial Freedom, Simon & Schuster, 2014, page 6

23. Bloomberg, "Student Debt,"

24. Ben Steverman, Bloomberg, "Half of Older Americans Have Nothing in Retirement Savings," March 26, 2019 https://www.

bloomberg.com/news/articles/2019-   03-26/
almost-half-of-older-americans-have-zero-in
retirement-savings.

About the Author

Erica Hill is a thought leader who coaches women on how to make, keep, and grow their money. She also teaches them how to ditch their fears surrounding money so that they can live life without limitations.

She is the author of *Money Management Strategies for Kids*, and co-author of *No More Chains*. She has been in the financial service industry for over twenty years and has experienced tremendous success.

Erica is the former owner of a mortgage company and currently owns a financial service agency. She is a sought-after empowerment and financial speaker that addresses the topics of personal growth and development, leadership, entrepreneurship, and wealth building. She is also the founder of a non-profit organization for youth development, which is dedicated to empowering youth on how to be well rounded, successful adults.

Erica realized that her story was meant to be shared to inspire others to seek financial wisdom and learn how to take control of their own destiny. She holds a Bachelor of Arts degree in Business Administration/Finance from Clark Atlanta University.

Made in the USA
Middletown, DE
19 January 2023

22565750R00033